Mysteries Revealed on Speaking in Tongues

TINA JACKSON

ISBN 978-1-63525-243-9 (Paperback)
ISBN 978-1-63525-244-6 (Digital)

Christian Faith Publishing, Inc.
296 Chestnut Street
Meadville, PA 16335
www.christianfaithpublishing.com

Printed in the United States of America

Thank you to Bible Gateway, www.biblegateway.com, for the reference of free scripture/Bibles available online. In scripture references, the italicized words are from Bible Gateway, omissions that were added in. Any bold font word is my emphasis. The vast majority of Bible scriptures are from the New King James Version unless noted otherwise.

Contents

How Did the Journey Begin?

"It is the glory of God to conceal a matter and the glory of kings to search a matter out" (Proverbs 25:2). God has many mysterious ways and hidden gems all laid out in the Word of God (the Bible). So let me tell you the mysteries He has unveiled to me about "why do we speak in tongues?"

There is more than the basic understanding of 1 Corinthians 14, where someone stands up in a church and gives a tongue and someone else follows up with an interpretation. Most churches think this is the only purpose for tongues, but there is much more. There is a personal prayer life of tongues that I will be unveiling through-out most of this book. Paul mentions about this personal prayer life in the last part of the statement from 1 Corinthians 14:28: "But if there is no interpreter, let him keep silent in church, **and let him speak to himself and to God.**" In addition, 1 Corinthians 14:39 states, "Therefore, brethren, desire earnestly to prophesy, and **do not forbid to speak with tongues.**" We will be going into more detailed personal prayer life of tongues and the church setting for tongues.

Let me start at the beginning of my journey. I was raised Catholic, and I was never taught anything about "speaking in tongues." So when I came across some charismatic Christians who I could tell were *different*, I wanted to know, "What is it that you got? Why are you so excited about God?" A Pentecostal mentor told me about the Holy Spirit, which consists of many things such as power (dynamite) and authority. When I first heard someone speaking in tongues in a church prayer meeting, I laughed and mocked those radical prayer warriors. Little did I understand the depths that they were tapping into the power source and heartbeat of God.

There were some basic principles of the word that I knew.

1. Satan wants to steal, kill, and destroy me and my family (John 10:10).
2. God gives good gifts (Matthew 7:11 and James 1:17).
3. I needed all the help I could get.

Even though I didn't understand the purpose of tongues, I knew there was something powerful about my mentor and those Pentecostals. So I said, "Bring it on! Give me the dynamite to blow Satan up." Through a simple prayer I just said, "Lord, fill me with your Holy Spirit to speak in tongues, in Jesus's name, amen." (Please note, the prerequisite is receiving Jesus as your Lord and Savior, which I had done seven months prior.) My mentor had told me, "You already have it. It's already in you. Whatever syllable you get, just start speaking it out even if it sounds foolish to you." So I did. I got a "Dah dah dah…" I spoke it out, but in my mind, I was think-ing, "What are you doing? This is stupid…" I had all kinds of things flying through my head. So day two in my morning prayer time, I said the same prayer, got the same syllables, and spoke them out; my mind started thinking crazy stuff, and I shut it down. Day three, Tuesday, June 17, 2003, same procedure. I began to roll my eyes with the "Dah, dah, dah" but before my eyes made the complete circle of a roll the "Dah, dah, dah" turned into *much* more! I began speaking an

Asian language and a few others. I was thrilled, overcome with tears of joy. My mind came into alignment and said, "wow! This is it!"

Little did I know, Satan (or one for his cohorts) sat down beside my glorious moment of agape love from God that was filling me. Satan whispered in my ear, "You don't know what you are saying." Check, you are right. "You don't know how to make it stop." At that moment, the language of the Lord was in full force and the once-glorious moment of joy turned to tears of panic and fright. I cried out to the Lord in my mind, "MAKE IT STOP!" Panic overtook me as Satan whispered the last deceptive lie, "You are possessed."

At that moment, I felt the strong arms of the Lord hold me tight with loving compassion, like a parent firmly hugging a terrified child. A *beautiful* and *soothing* song began to sing through my voice (Zephaniah 3:17). It was so soft and comforting. As the Lord rocked me side to side, gently saying, "Shhhhhhh, it's okay. I will never hurt you. I love you." I felt AGAPE LOVE fill me again. The tears that started off as tears of joy that turned to tears of terror and panic ceased and comfort and gladness filled me afresh. As I write this portion, tears flood back to me, because God is a loving Father and He doesn't like His children being lied to/deceived. Satan tried to pervert a very glorious moment, but through that experience, I felt the arms of the Lord holding me, rocking me, and singing a sweet song to me.

This led me on a journey of asking the Lord, "Why do we speak in tongues?" Little did I know the mysterious revealed are oh so beautiful!

Scriptures referenced, New King James Version (NKJV)

Proverbs 25:2 *It is* the glory of God to conceal a matter,
But the glory of kings *is* to search out a matter.

Zephaniah 3:17: The LORD your God in your midst,
The Mighty One, will save;
He will rejoice over you with gladness,
He will quiet *you* with His love,
He will rejoice over you with singing."

Matthew 7:11 If you then, being evil, know how to give good gifts to your children, how much more will your Father who is in heaven give good things to those who ask Him!

John 10:10 The thief does not come except to steal, and to kill, and to destroy. I have come that they may have life, and that they may have *it* more abundantly.

James 1:17 Every good gift and every perfect gift is from above, and comes down from the Father of lights, with whom there is no variation or shadow of turning.

Navajo Indians

As I began to work in my prayer language, a certain phrase would continually repeat over and over and over. It was annoying! I can't recall the whole phrase now, but it had the word *keyah* in it. (I didn't know the correct spelling back then.) I went on an intensive search with trying to look words up and asking people who spoke different languages if they knew what I was saying. I had no success, and I knew I wasn't praying for a Kia car. So I continued on with my prayer language; often that one phrase would start repeating over and over. UGH!

Like a sassy teenager with attitude, I inquired of the Lord... "Lord, what is this? I ask for interpretation. I KNOW this means something. You say to 'ask and you shall receive' (Matthew 7:8), I'm asking! What does this mean? You also say the Holy Spirit within will interpret tongues, interpret my tongue! Why aren't you answering me! There is nothing on the world wide web, and I KNOW this means something." After three weeks of research, I gave up trying to figure it out.

Nine months from the time it started, I was in my closet putting clothes away when a Christian TV show was playing. They began to say some of the key words in the phrase I had prayed. I came running to the TV, but the show was over, and I missed the contact information. This was back in 2004, so there wasn't DVRs where I could rewind and find out what the show was. We didn't even have cable at the time; we just had an antenna. I said, "Lord, bring that around again, if that was what I think it was."

The next day, I was going about my day and a different show was on. The Christian channel mentions some of the key words in their show too. Again, I missed the details and asked the Lord a second time… "Lord, bring that around again. I know I am hearing this right."

The third day, I was at my kitchen table and another show came on with the similar information (different time of day from the last two). I wrote everything down and went to my computer. It was about missionaries going to the Navajo Indians and a great revival was breaking out, because many Navajo's were coming to Christ.

As I went through the website, there was a dialectic button. I clicked on it and listened to the Navajo Indian language. Sure enough, THAT WAS THE SAME LANGUAGE I'VE BEEN PRAYING FOR ABOUT NINE MONTHS off and on! I researched some more and got a plethora of information about the culture. I found a few of the words I was praying; for instance, *keyah* means land. On and on the words were translated; it was overwhelming. Once I got a moment to take it all in, anger came over me. I went to my kitchen table (my prayer room), slammed my hand on the table, and yelled aggressively at the bay window to God, "PRAYER MEETING RIGHT NOW!" Many people think, "You talk to God like that? Wow." It's not "right" per se, but I was angry, and I wanted answers, and we are family. Family is raw at times.

I said, "You know I asked you some nine months ago what these words meant and I searched these words and nothing… nothing came up! Now, there is a ton of information. What is up with that?!"

The Spirit of the Lord answered, "Tina, if I would have told you what you were praying about in Navajo Indian, you would have prayed it in English. I needed you to pray it in Navajo Indian.

Everything is birthed into the spiritual realm first, 'Light Be,' light was. When you spoke the words I gave you, those words went out into the atmosphere. The Navajo Indians heard it in the spiritual realm, that is why when the missionaries got there, they received Jesus. They already 'heard' it. My word does not return void, but it WILL go forth and accomplish what it is sent forth to do (Isaiah 55:11). This is what it means to be blessed to be a blessing to the nations (Genesis 22:18). The Navajo nation was blessed by your obedience to my word. Yes, it is your mouth and you allowed me to speak through you. We co-labor together" (1 Corinthians 3:9).

At that moment, I clunked my head on the kitchen table, face down, and said, "You are God and I am not. Your ways are higher. Your thoughts are not my thoughts. I don't care to ever know again what I am praying. It is all good." I was humbled very much before the Lord that day, but His gladness and joy covered me and I felt honored to now be a part of the big picture.

To put even more icing on the cake, I told my pastor (at the time) the experience about praying for missionaries going to the Navajo Indians and how the Navajo Indians were being radically transformed. That weekend at church, a couple stood up and said, "We have sold everything we have and we are going to be missionaries for a Navajo Indian region." Wow! I was about to jump out of my skin with joy! I was praying for them to hear the call too and didn't even know it! Wow! It is so awesome to see God work in multiple ways right before your eyes. I could sense God's joy as well.

I encourage you, when you are praying in tongues and it seems like a phrase starts repeating over and over and over again, continue to press on. Press into that prayer language. The Lord showed me it's like a hammer breaking a brick wall down with each repeated phrase. Since that breakthrough, I have not repeated that one phrase ever since then. At the time, I was able to repeat the phrase to someone, because the Spirit would give me utterance. But nowadays, I only remember a teeny tiny portion of the phrase. The Holy Spirit knows just what to work on. We give voice to the mysteries. God has always been faithful to answer me when I've asked, "What does this mean?" Indeed, it may take some time (like nine months) but He has ALWAYS answered me. ☺

Never give up. Some things just need to be hammered done in the spiritual realm. It reminds me of a scripture from Jeremiah 23:29 (AMP), "Is not My word like a fire [that consumes all that cannot endure the test]? says the Lord, and like a hammer that breaks in pieces the rock [of most stubborn resistance]?"

Scriptures referenced, New King James Version (NKJV)

Genesis 22:18 "In your seed all the nations of the earth shall be blessed, because you have obeyed My voice."

Isaiah 55:11 So shall My word be that goes forth from My mouth;
It shall not return to Me void,
But it shall accomplish what I please,
And it shall prosper *in the thing* for which I sent it.

Matthew 7:8 For everyone who asks receives, and he who seeks finds, and to him who knocks it will be opened.

1 Corinthians 3:9 For we are God's fellow workers; you are God's field, *you are* God's building.

Praying for Challenging Family Members

Have you ever had someone you needed to pray for that just "annoyed" you or "hurt you"? That is a challenge. I had that happen to me on a few occasions. The first time I was faced with such a challenge was from the reading of my grandmother's will. My Grandma Grace held a special place in my heart, and I in hers. We were close from beginning to end. Grandma was the one to teach me how to cook, clean, paint, sew, and so much more. As a teenager, I would visit with her almost every weekend, then in my twenties and thirties, my family and Grandma/pa would go to their cabin up north and my husband and I would help them out. There were very few weekends that we didn't spend together. A few years before her life was coming to a close, we would speak to each other daily, even if it was a quick five-minute check in call. Upon my grandmother's death, she willed me a portion of her investment that my mom felt she should have gotten all of it. My grandmother also put a clause in her will that my husband and I have first choice to buy the farm. (We would have to buy out my mom and two brothers, but we get first choice.) This angered my mother beyond words and my brothers were in an uproar as well. I thought, "Really? Haven't you seen our relationship for the last thirty-five-plus years? When is the last time you came up north to help out?"

Needless to say, things got nasty. My mom's bitterness, rage, anger, and resentment stewed so much we had to separate from each other for a while. In the mornings, I would do my prayer cards. On each card was someone's name and what to pray about for that person. Well…when it came to my mom's card, I didn't want to write or say anything in English. My conversation with the Lord was something like this: "Lord, I know they (my mom and brothers) don't understand what they are doing (being so hurtful and mean). I don't want to pray in English over them, because I don't want any ill feelings to taint my prayers over them. I give them to you. I only want to pray in tongues over them, because I know that it will be the perfect will of God being prayed over them." I flung my wrist as if I had a Frisbee in my hand and flicked it to God.

Each day, I would get my prayer cards out and pray. As my mom and my brother's cards would come up, tongues would be the only thing you'd hear. About nine months goes by and I'm at the gym teaching a fitness class. (By the way that was an awesome job; you get paid to exercise!) After class, I started a conversation with one of my Catholic students and telling him about the baptism of the Holy Spirit to speak in tongues. He is from overseas, somewhere near Israel and was excited to partake in the gift to speak in tongues. I lead him through a prayer, and I softly start speaking in tongues while I waited for him to start speaking. A moment goes by and he says, "Tina, do you know what you are saying?"

I smiled and said, "No, but it's okay. I don't need to know. It's all good." (If you read the Navajo chapter, you understand why I was at peace with not knowing.) As I was smiling at him, he says, "Well, I do know what you are saying." My eyebrows lifted; I looked star struck.

I said, "Well, enlighten me. What am I saying?"

He says, "You are speaking Hebrew, Aramaic, and German. I don't know German, but I know you are speaking German. In Hebrew and Aramaic, you are praying for your mom and your brother or brothers. You are crying out for your mom and saying 'mom, mother, mommy' and all the different ways. And you are reverencing the Lord like the Jews do. You know like us Catholics do? We have certain prayers we pray. The Jews have certain prayers they pray and you are praying them! You are praying about the Sabbath..." By this time, I was balling my eyes out and in desperate need of a Kleenex! Through my tears, I laughed and said, "I'm supposed to be ministering to you, not you ministering to me. I'm so sorry." I was in no condition to help him receive speaking in tongues.

He laughed, hugged me, and said, "It's okay. I have a Pentecostal friend overseas, and I leave tomorrow. I will seek him out to help me, okay?" I smiled, broke down in tears again, because I KNEW God surprised me with this awesome interpretation to encourage me on. I felt such a love from God come over me, because my student knew nothing of my personal life and he unfolded so much in a matter of a few minutes. I left the gym in hopes of finding someone who spoke German, just to confirm there wasn't something more.

Not long after that unveiling, our family was traveling to Wisconsin to visit some relatives, and we stopped for the night in the Upper Peninsula of Michigan to rest. At the lobby desk was a worker and somehow we got to talking and she said she spoke German. I got so excited! I said, "I've been told I'm speaking some German, can you tell me what I'm saying?"

She said, "Sure." She listened and said, "Well… you are speaking other languages too, but in German you are praying for your mom and brother or brothers…" and she went on and on. I was ecstatic! I thanked her, told her briefly about the baptism of the Holy Spirit, and went on my way to my room.

I inquired of the Lord, "Why are you showing me this stuff about my mom and brothers?" No response yet. About six more weeks goes by and I got a call from my mom, "Tina, you know those 'tongues' you have been telling me about for years? I got them today! And I rededicated my heart to Jesus..." I was so thrilled for my mom! What a huge step of faith.

On top of that, my daughter, Alexis, woke up one Sunday and said, "Mom, you MUST call Uncle Bob and get him to church today."

I laughed. "Yah, well that will be a miracle." My birth family was raised Catholic, and our family went to an Assembly of God church, which was totally different then the ritual/routine type of service. Alexis was very persistent and said, "YOU MUST CALL HIM!"

I said, "Okay." That was odd for her to be so persistent about God things, so I didn't want to miss out on anything. I called him and he said, "Sure, I'll meet you at the church." I was blown off my chair. He was awakened to a new form of church that day. The pastor preached a message that was identical to what was going on in his life at the time, which I'm sure really ministered to him. After service he turned to me and said, "You set me up!"

I didn't know if he was mad or laughing inside, so I lightheartedly, with a laugh, said, "No, I didn't. God did and Alexis was the one who heard from God, so blame them." ☺ I do not know the extent of what happened in his heart that day, but I know it was good, because God is good.

I went to the Lord about the two breakthroughs with my mom and one brother. Why the three languages? This is what to Lord said to me that day: "Tina, I honor you." At that moment, I felt a crown placed on my head (Psalm 8:5). With agape love consuming me and tears in my eyes, I said, "Wait, no... I HONOR YOU!" (I thought, surely the Lord has this backward). In the Lord's loving tone, He continued, "Tina, I honor you. You casted your care upon me for your mother and brothers. I wanted you to know that I am diligently working on things. I gave the three different languages because with two or three witnesses My Word is established (2 Corinthians 13:1). The one gentlemen knew two, and the other, the third language. I wanted you to know, you can 'Rest' (a Sabbath) in me to know, I will work all things out for good (Romans 8:28)".

Ohhh... what a glorious day that was—to find out we can "rest" in the Lord; cast our cares on him and he WILL perform the work. We give voice (His language—tongues), and He does the work. We co-labor together. We work together to bring people to salvation. I have found this type of prayer for challenging people to be most beneficial, because it keeps you (me) in holiness, so our feelings don't hinder effective prayers.

I encourage you today, pray in tongues for the people you don't know how to pray for. God knows EXACTLY what they need. The Holy Spirit will intercede on your behalf and pray things out with groaning and spiritual knowledge to get things accomplished (Romans 8:27-28).

Scriptures referenced, New King James Version (NKJV)

Psalm 8:5 For You have made him a little lower than the angels, And You have crowned him with glory and honor.

Romans 8:26–27 Likewise the Spirit also helps in our weaknesses. For we do not know what we should pray for as we ought, but the Spirit Himself makes intercession for us with groanings which cannot be uttered. [27] Now He who searches the hearts knows what the mind of the Spirit *is,* because He makes intercession for the saints according to *the will of* God.

Romans 8:28 And we know that all things work together for good to those who love God, to those who are the called according to *His* purpose.

2 Corinthians 13:1 This *will be* the third *time* I am coming to you. "By the mouth of two or three witnesses every word shall be established."

Bikers, Tattoos, and Demons

I need to start you off with some background information. As a newbie Christian on fire for the Lord, I was reading various books and studying the Bible for hours at a time. My fire for the Lord was flaming hot! I was led to read a book by Benny Hinn, called *Good Morning, Holy Spirit*. I found the book very interesting, and it was feeding my spirit man. One day, I came across a chapter or mention on demons. I laughed at the thought of demons existing today because my Catholic upbringing never discussed such a topic. As I mockingly laughed, I tossed the book like a Frisbee across the room, saying, "Yah, right!" and went about my day.

Since I was still wanting to do "whatever" the Lord would have me to do, the Lord put me up for a challenge. He began to lead me to Bikers. I dreaded bikers! I feared bikers with everything in me.

The Lord asked me, "Why are you so scared of them?"

I said, "It's the tattoos. The leather jackets, the loud bikes..."

He said, "You wear a black leather jacket. The leather is to protect them when riding. It's not to make them look mean. As for the tattoos... YOU have a tattoo."

I said, "But my tattoo is covered. No one can see it and it's not scary like some with snakes, hell, death, Satan, etc. And as for my jacket... well... I feel safe in black leather."

He said, "Tina, it's nothing to be afraid of. Most of them who have tattoos are just wearing their feelings on the outside. Therefore, it is easier for you to minister to them." I never thought of it like that. He said, "You can read them and see the root of the situation (in most circumstances)."

I was like "Wow! Cool!" So my adventure began with the bikers and tattoos.

My first encounter was at the eye doctor's office. A man sat beside me in shorts with a scary fire burning hell skull on his leg. I looked at it intensively. I looked at him with an excitement in my voice and a smile on my face as I stared him in the eyes and laughingly said, "So... are you looking forward to burning in hell? Where you are tormented day and night and night and day and there is no relief?"

His mouth dropped. His eyes widened, and his head tilted forward. I held strong to my gaze, lifted my eyebrows and tilted my head slightly to the side and closed my teeth smile to a slight grin as I awaited an answer. He took a deep gasp and said, "wow! If I wasn't saved, I don't know how I would have answered that question!"

Oh the *RELIEF* that came over me to know he was saved made me exhale in a long "swoooh." He said, "I got saved a few years ago, but these are permanent, so it is what it is."

I said, "Thank God you're saved, because I was trying to overcome my fear of people with tattoos and I have no idea where I was going with that." We laughed and I was taken to the second encounter.

Encounter 2 happened while in Orlando, Florida, at the Walt Disney World Wilderness Lodge in the elevator. The Lord purposely had me wait in the elevator for this one gentleman to step in. (I was going to go up myself to my floor, but the Lord said, "Wait for him. Don't close the doors yet.") In Florida, it's hot. He has his tank top and shorts on. I do not recall now if it was his forearms or his legs, but one side of his body had praying hands and the other limb had a burning skull like hell. I tilted my head to observe and said, "Looks like you have a conflict of interest going on. Are you on heaven's side or hell's side?"

He said, "My uncle was a praying man and sought the Lord, and I miss him. This one [hell] is because I think it looks cool."

I said, "I'd go with your uncle's choice unless you like the thought of being tormented day and night and night and day." I said the last part with great evil in my voice. His eyes widened. I asked, "Have you given your heart to the Lord Jesus yet?"

He said, "No." his floor came forth, and he was in a hurry to get off.

As his stepped off the elevator, I said, "Why don't you make today the day and choose your uncle's way, Jesus's way?" The elevator doors closed. I was so excited to be overcoming my fear of tattoos and biker-looking people. So time to graduate to the next level.

Level 3: I'm in a church denomination that is not Pentecostal (not a tongue-talking church), doesn't work much in the gifts of the spirit, and is spiritually dead. (Please know, they love God and the community with all their heart. They were very good people and feed the community, so on and so forth, but when it comes to spiritual gifts, they were lacking and I was a baby Christian with NO spiritual exposure except from what I was reading in books by Benny Hinn, Smith Wigglesworth, Lester Sumrall, Kenneth Hagin Sr., the Copelands, etc.) Anyways, there was an acquaintance at the church whose brother got in a motorcycle accident and was in a coma. I was in prayer over him one Friday morning (this was the seventh day he was in the coma). The Lord put upon my heart to call my acquaintance. It was 8:00 AM, and I asked if I could come to the hospital and pray for her brother.

As she said, "Yah, sure." Right then, a power-packed prayer came upon me, "And your brother is going to rise up from that stooper sleep, ARISE! AWAKEN! NOW in Jesus's name, amen..." I was stunned by the words coming out of my mouth. That was not how this church body prayed (prayers for this church was, "Lord, if it be thy will...")

"Okay, see you later."

As the time came, I was fired up! I was pumped up, because I could feel the presence of the Lord. I was walking tall with authority and a stride. I headed for the ICU area. I turned the corner and walked into a large room filled with *BIKERS*! Black leather *EVERYWHERE*! Tattoos of evil everywhere and my heart skips a beat. As I scan the room, no acquaintance either. I felt like I walked into the lion's den. With a long exhale, I look at the hospital bed and I see the young man (maybe about nineteen years old) in the bed and awake! Oh, the joy that leaped within me to see him awake. I thought "Mission accomplished, it's time to go!" Yah... that was the moment God got His laugh in and said, "Watch this angels. Hehehe." ☺

The mother of the boy says, "Around 8:00 AM, my son and the girl next door in the other room both woke up from their comas." I knew that prayer went forth that morning at that time and with much excitement, as I was standing at the foot of his bed, I shouted, "PRAISE GOD!" Well... that started the ruckus. The boy in the bed, who thankfully was strapped down, starts belching and talking in an evil tone with beady eyes, "Prayers do not work!" over and over and over. Oh, at that moment, I dreaded throwing that Benny Hinn book across the floor. I needed to know what to do and didn't have any idea how this would end. The regret within me was deep for mocking God's servant and His word. As I swallowed hard, my fear mixed with anger turned toward God. So as this boy is now farting, belching, speaking evil over and over and sweating profusely (drips,

I mean drips of sweat pouring off his face), "Prayers do not work!" Oh, and don't forget all the bikers in the room who are freaking out now too. I decide I am going to have a conversation with God in my head. "YOU TRICKED ME! I thought I was coming here to pray for a boy to arise from a coma and this is clearly a demon!" I'm freaked out to say the least.

The Lord says, "Tina... he can't see you. He sees Jesus. You have your armor on." My eyebrows rose up and I thought, "That's a good thing he doesn't see Tina, because Tina wants to run out of here!" And with that one statement from the Lord, the Lord reminded me of Ephesians 6:10–18 (NKJV):

> [10]Finally, my brethren, be strong in the Lord and in the power of His might. [11]Put on the whole armor of God, that you may be able to stand against the wiles of the devil. [12]For we do not wrestle against flesh and blood, but against principalities, against powers, against the rulers of the darkness of this age, against spiritual *hosts* of wickedness in the heavenly *places*. [13]Therefore take up the whole armor of God, that you may be able to withstand in the evil day, and having done all, to stand.
>
> [14]Stand therefore, having girded your waist with truth, having put on the breastplate of righteousness, [15]and having shod your feet with the preparation of the gospel of peace; [16]above all, taking the shield of faith with which you will be able to quench all the fiery darts of the wicked one. [17]And take the helmet of salvation, and the sword of the Spirit, which is the word of God;

¹⁸**praying always with all prayer and suppli-cation in the Spirit**, being watchful to this end with all perseverance and supplication for all the saints—

I knew within me... "I got my armor on. NOW, **pray in the Holy Spirit** [tongues]." A boldness rose up in me from *deep* within. My eyes turned to determination and compassion for the boy. When that happened, the evil spirit began to say through him (he is still farting, belching, sweating, and speaking in an evil tone), "I got to get out of here. I got to get out of here..."

I thought "You are darn right, YOU HAVE TO GET OUT OF HERE IN JESUS'S NAME!" Oh... the boldness of walking in the Spirit is so *awesome*! So *empowering*! I LOVE IT!

With all the chaos going on, people were running around. The mother apologized to me, "I don't know what's wrong with him. He's not like this. I'm so sorry." She continually tried to calm him down. The bikers are off their chairs and standing around in awe. Finally, the nurse came in and asked us all to leave a moment so he can "relieve" himself. I thought, *Okay... good time to regroup and chat with the Lord, because my acquaintance is still not there yet.*

I decided to look over to the little girl who woke up that morn-ing, and to my surprise, the Lord showed me a demon sitting on top of this nine-year-old's chest, choking her. With her neck arched, she was gasping for breath and a naked imp-looking thing (similar to the imp in the movie, *Lord of the Rings*) was on top of her, as her father is patting the little girl's shoulder, "Shhh, try to relax".

Tears filled my eyes... I cried out to the Lord in my head, "Lord, this is too much! I don't know what I'm doing. I threw the book! I got my pampers on. I got bikers! Tattoos! Demons!" As I was try-ing to have a pity party overload, my acquaintance and her husband showed up. I felt like help arrived, "THERE'S HOPE."

Not many weeks prior, I had prayed with the acquaintance's husband, Jeff, to receive the Holy Spirit. He was my first person I ever prayed with to receive the baptism of the Holy Spirit. He did receive, and so I knew he spoke in tongues. We needed all the help we could get, so I said, "We are going to go in there to pray for your brother to be of sound mind and healed. Jeff, you pray in tongues and only tongues. You [the acquaintance], you pray in English for your brother and I'm going to pray in tongues too." Keep in mind, this couple had no idea what just happened in the room and I did not have the heart to say, "Oh, by the way, your brother is possessed by a demon."

We headed into the room because they called us back. With boldness, we took our positions. The sister by his side, Jeff at the foot of the bed, and me with my hand on the boy's back, standing beside him. The boy is doing the same thing as before: farting, sweating, and belching in evil tone, "I got to get out of here." We prayed for about five to ten minutes and BAM! It broke. I just *knew* he was set free. There was peace in the room. I was excited because "mission WAS complete" at that moment. We said our good-byes, and I left.

As I left, I looked once again to the little girl's room. This time, I saw nothing disturbing. There was peace, so I left the hospital with a wealth of information and experience. I replayed the situation over and over in my mind and always felt regretful that I didn't step into the little girl's room. I cried much for her, hoping she was well. I was so comforted by the Lord one day, "Tina, just as when you prayed at 8:00 AM and she woke up from that coma, when you prayed in the other room in tongues, I took care of the demon in her room that is why you saw PEACE. It's okay. She's fine. There is no distance in the spirit realm." I was glad to hear that.

Oh, the story isn't over yet... ☺ That was all on a Friday. On Sunday, my acquaintance came running up to me. She said, "Tina, I went to visit my brother on Saturday and he sat up in bed, looked me in the eyes, and said, 'Sis, tell me about your Jesus.' I was able to lead my brother to the LORD!" Glory to God! Tears still fill my eyes every time I tell that story. God is so good. When people are set free from evil influences, they can hear the gospel. Praise God.

The boy came to church a couple weeks later after he was released from the hospital. He shook my hand and with a shaking chin as he fought tears, he said, "Thank you." Oh, how obedience is better than sacrifice (1 Samuel 15:22). That boy was set free and saved due to obedience. When the Lord tells you to "Go," just go. There is something so glorious to see and partake in that words just cannot describe.

I thought God got the last laugh on my biker/demon fear of throwing the book... No... He had to top that by some years later, when I got an invitation to preach/teach about this topic, "The Mysteries Revealed on Speaking in Tongues." As my first ever invitation, which is always a big deal for someone who wants to tell the good news... it was at a *BIKER CHURCH*! No kidding! I shook my head in disgust at His humor. I just felt Him laughing at my fear.

As I squinted my eyes, crimped my lips with playful banter, I said, "Sure, I'll come to your church." And so I did. It was another test of faith as the main pastor of the church was late coming to the meeting. As I am telling my testimonies, I hear about ten loud, roaring bikes pull into the parking lot as they all walk in with their tattoos and black leather... I just had to laugh *with* the Lord, "You got my back, Lord. I have no intension of mocking you ever again. I love you too. I feel your protection and presence, thank you." ☺

I hope you get to *experience* God as a *daddy*, a *friend*, a *teacher*, a *helper*, and so much more. He does have a sense of humor, and He wants all your fears to be gone as stated in 2 Timothy 1:7, "For God did not give you a spirit of fear, but of power, love and a sound mind."

Never fear demons. Keep your armor on and they will only see Jesus. Keep renewed in your mind over what God says *is* true. You will be more than a conqueror (Romans 8:37). As I studied about demons sometime later, I noticed in the Bible that demons are usually loud and obnoxious; bind those spirits. Take your authority over them, as the Lord has instructed you to do in His word in Matthew 16:19 "And I will give you the keys of the kingdom of heaven, and whatever you bind on earth will be bound in heaven, and whatever you loose on earth will be loosed in heaven." Also, bind the strong man as in Mark 3:27 "No one can enter a strong man's house and plunder his goods, unless he first binds the strong man. And then he will plunder his house."

Just keep it simple… If you don't know what to do, pray in tongues and let the Holy Spirit give utterance. ☺

"The Holy Spirit proceeds from God himself" (John 15:26).

Scriptures referenced, various translations

1 Samuel 15:22 (New Living Translation)
But Samuel replied, "What is more pleasing to the LORD:
your burnt offerings and sacrifices
or your obedience to his voice?
Listen! Obedience is better than sacrifice,
and submission is better than offering the fat of rams.

Romans 8:37 (New King James Version)
Yet in all these things we are more than conquerors through Him who loved us.

Infirmities, Come Out

A little background information for the next testimony: My eldest daughter, Alexis, was baptized in the Holy Spirit (spoke in tongues) around the age of five. One day, she came home from church and was speaking in tongues. I called the youth pastor and asked what happened at church that day. She said they released the baptism of the Holy Spirit. We rejoiced together as I told her, "Well, Alexis is speaking in tongues!" Amen.

For about two weeks, Alexis was playing around with speaking in tongues and then just stopped. I was concerned. She had no interest in wanting to do it anymore.

About one year later, my youngest daughter, Amanda, got filled with the Holy Spirit, and she began speaking in tongues. I was thrilled all over again. This time, I was determined to keep her working in it. At bedtime, we would play a game. We would each hold a stuffed animal and begin talking in tongues back and forth to each other, as if the stuffed animals were talking. We would sometimes get deep belly aching laughs because some of the languages we spoke sounded pure "funny." We would sing songs in tongues and have a great time together. I inquired of the Lord if we were using the Holy Spirit (tongues) in an adulterous way, and I sensed the Lord say, "I like to have fun and play too." I had the greatest peace from seeing an image of the Lord Jesus laughing with us, as we heard languages/

songs come forth that were so funny to us. He was laughing, because we were taking such great delight. Just like a parent laughs and takes great delight in seeing their child laugh at something so simple like a peekaboo. So Amanda kept her tongue languages.

Fast forward six to seven years. Alexis is almost twelve years old, and I was teaching the girls about "needing to seek your own relationship with the Lord." I knew they were getting of age where they will need to take responsibility for their own walk with the Lord and in building a personal relationship with Him. I was trying to teach that all along, but I felt like they weren't getting it.

One day, Alexis came down with a fever, 103 to 104 degrees Fahrenheit. We prayed, and the fever didn't break. This was unheard of in our household. We would rebuke a fever (in Jesus's name) and instantly they were gone. We were perplexed by this infirmity. I broke down and went to the store and bought medicine, because I hated seeing my daughter ill and didn't know what else *to do*. Three days of this fever and lethargic spirit (was there a concern arising within me? Sure there was). On the third day, she was sitting at the kitchen table moaning and groaning, head down, and looked awful. I took her temperature almost 104 degrees still! UGH! I poured her some medicine, and she didn't take it, so I placed it before her.

She looked up and said, "Mom, you have such a good relationship with Jesus, tell Him to heal me. Why isn't He healing me?"

That statement struck a cord with me. Anger came over me. I smacked my hand on the table, looked at her, and said, "Get off my shirt tails and get your own relationship with the Lord and PRAY IN TONGUES!" and I walked away. Maybe that isn't the way you should talk to someone who is sick, but I was telling her for months that she needs to go to the Lord herself and that statement rubbed me wrong.

As I sat down to look at e-mails, just a few feet away so I would cool down, I heard tongues. Since Amanda was sitting with us, I assumed it was her. Then I hear Amanda say, "Mom, Mom... Alexis is praying in tongues!" I turned around, and sure enough, she was letting it rip. We all started rejoicing and having a tongue talking party as we danced around the kitchen. Then all of a sudden, with a bright and cheery countenance, Alexis says to Amanda, "Come on, Amanda, let's go play!" With a skip in her step and joy in her heart, they took off upstairs to play.

About two hours go by and Alexis comes down for a drink of water. It dawned on me that she was so well. Her countenance and energy were back in full strength. I said, "Alexis, come here." I took her temperature, 98.7, perfect! I looked at the table; the medicine was still in the cup. I said, "Alexis, do you see now? Praying in tongues quickens your mortal body." With that, she did what a kid sometimes does, "Ok, Mom... later!" Without a second thought, she was back upstairs, playing.

In the book of Jude verse 20 (amplified, it says) "But you, beloved, build yourselves up [founded] on your most holy faith [make progress, rise like an edifice higher and higher], praying in the Holy Spirit." Couple that with Romans 8:11, "And if the Spirit of Him Who raised up Jesus from the dead dwells in you, [then] He Who raised up Christ *Jesus* from the dead will also restore to life your mortal (short-lived, perishable) bodies through His Spirit Who dwells in you."

When you pray in the Holy Spirit (which consists of tongues-the language of God and angels) it quickens your mortal body. That life-giving substance that raised Christ from the dead dwells in every believer. We activate that healing through believing, declaring, praying in tongues, or sometimes by receiving a touch from another believer. It is awesome to have access to such a wonderful life-giving power!

Russia

As I go through my daily walk with the Lord, I harken to His voice because He is continually teaching me things—whether I am in the shower, on the throne, driving the car, waiting in line at a store, or wherever. I am always awaiting His voice. One day, I was home alone walking through my house, minding my own business, and the Lord prompted me to *urgently* pray. As I began to pray, I heard Russian. Now, I don't know Russian, but I knew that the language was Russian. As Russian spoke through me, my heart began to break and I was feeling *GREAT* sorrow, I asked the Lord, "What is going on?"

He said, "Shhhh, JUST PRAY!" All I knew was something was tragically wrong.

After twenty minutes of heart-wrenching tears and Russian prayer, the Spirit of the Lord lifted, and I felt peace. Off and on for the next two weeks, "PRAY!" Again, Russian would come forth. I questioned but did not pursue the "need to know what was going on" because of the prior experiences. I knew that God's ways are higher, so I rested in that truth, but I was curious as to the urgencies of these prayers.

As I sat at the kitchen table in prayer one morning (two weeks after the Russian started), the Lord said, "Turn on the TV." When I did, it was the news. Upon turning on the TV and it was the weather,

I rolled my eyes in sarcasm toward the Lord like "Really? Thanks for letting me know how to dress the kids for the day." But right after weather was not traffic or sports; it was "Here are the miracle children from the Russian school bombing."

As they panned the camera through the hospital ward, people were giving testimony (translated), "God saved my child… God this… God that… God… God…" I was floored! One testimony after another about God on public TV! I was so excited as my mouth hung open and I felt the presence of the Lord sit to the right of me. He said, "Tina, this is what you were a part of." I felt so honored and humbled at the same time. Then He said something that rocked me to the core. He said, "If you didn't pray it, I could not have done it."

I said, "What?"

He repeated again, "If you didn't pray it, I could not have done it." I was baffled.

With that, He began to give me the revelation:

"Tina, where am I?"

"Well, you are everywhere, Lord."

His response, "No, I am not. Let me help you. Our Father who art in _____?"

"Oh… heaven."

He continued, "And where is Jesus?"

"He's seated at the right hand of the Father and the earth is his footstool."

The Lord then questioned, "Where are you?"

"I'm in the Earth."

"Who is the Prince of the Earth?"

"Satan,… that is why Jesus came to get the keys back but people need to change citizenship" (Ephesians 2:2).

The revelation continued with the Holy Spirit was here on the earth hovering over the surface of the water. After Jesus's resurrection, the Holy Spirit then came to make His abode within people. Jesus commissioned people to "wait" for the Holy Spirit to come upon them—UP out of their belly and *ON* them through their vocal cords = UPON. When the Holy Spirit is "received" *within* and allowed to come upon, a shield of protection comes upon us. As we speak in tongues, it is God's language. We can harken to Him and give voice into the atmosphere as the Spirit leads. God knows what needs to get done. As He said, "Light be," and light was, so it is likewise. When He prompts us to pray, He is speaking through us to change the atmosphere. The words that came out in Russian were life-giving words.

The Lord continued on and said, "This is what it means to have the blessings of Abraham. Nations are blessed through you. Russia was blessed through your obedience to give voice to My Word. My word *will not* return void. It *will* accomplish what/where I send it. Thank you. Thank you for allowing Me to flow through you. We co-labor together."

As He continued on, I began to cry because I heard and felt Him cry, "I just wish my children would pray My language. I know what needs to get done, but I need a voice." Through the tears, I promised the Lord I would do what I could to help explain to the body of Christ the importance of tongues.

You see, we are ambassadors for the Lord. In 1 Corinthians 5:20 "Now then, we are ambassadors for Christ, as though God were pleading through us: we implore *you* on Christ's behalf, be reconciled to God." According to the *Merriam-Webster Dictionary, ambassador* means "the highest-ranking person who represents his or her own government while living in another country."[1]

We are to represent the kingdom of heaven here on earth. God wants His kingdom to come, His *will* to be done on earth as it is in heaven. We are the little "g" gods/children of God that do the Father's will (Psalm 82:6). It is a lovely partnership. God oversees everything. We just rest and give voice to what His wants said. It is awesome!

He had me get a piece of paper to draw this all out. I would suggest you do likewise to help you get the revelation, even though this revelation goes deeper than the tongues revelation. It gives you a great picture to mediate on the Lord equipping the saints. Draw a circle to represent earth. Then draw God (LOVE) in heaven (a big heart is good); Jesus at the right hand, seated with his feet resting on the earth (Acts 7:49 and other places). Now draw yourself in the Earth and the Holy Spirit surrounding you. Draw Satan in the Earth with him flinging arrows toward you. See your Holy Spirit shield protecting you.

It was such an honor and privilege to be in the United States and yet in the spirit help Russia and work with God Almighty, Jesus, and the Holy Spirit to do such a great mission. The book of John chapters 14 and 15 are so great to mediate on, but let me point to you John 14:10–12.

> Do you not believe that I am in the Father, and the Father in Me? **The words that I speak to you I do not speak on My own *authority*; but the Father who dwells in Me does the works**.[11] Believe Me that I *am* in the Father and the Father in Me, or else believe Me for the sake of the works themselves.[12] Most assuredly, I say to you, he who believes in Me, **the works that I do he will do also; and greater *works*** than these he will do, because I go to My Father.

There is so much in this scripture I pray the Holy Spirit gives you the revelation to *really* get it. In John 17:21, the scripture discusses how we are one as they are one. So don't think it odd that God needs you and wants to work through you. He has to work with and through people. He is in heaven. Earth is not heaven yet. We are the in Earth. We have the Holy Spirit to lead, guide, and direct our steps to help bring the kingdom of heaven to earth. Isn't that beautiful? Amen and amen. While praying in tongues, you give voice to the Spirit of the Lord (His language) and watch God do the signs, wonders, and miracles (Mark 16:20).

Scriptures referenced, New King James Version (NKJV)

Psalm 82:6 I said, "You *are* gods,
And all of you *are* children of the Most High.

Mark 16:20 And they went out and preached everywhere, the Lord working with *them* and confirming the word through the accompanying signs. Amen.

John 17:21 That they all may be one, as You, Father, *are* in Me, and I in You; that they also may be one in Us, that the world may believe that You sent Me.

Acts 7:49 Heaven *is* My throne,
And earth *is* My footstool.
What house will you build for Me? says the LORD,
Or what *is* the place of My rest?

Ephesians 2:2 (New Living Translation)
You used to live in sin, just like the rest of the world, obeying the devil—the commander of the powers in the unseen world. He is the spirit at work in the hearts of those who refuse to obey God.

Taming the Tongue

When I got born again in 2002 (received Jesus as my Lord and Savior) and filled with the Holy Spirit in June 2003 (asked the Holy Spirit to manifest in and through me), there was a lot of purging that needed to happen in my life. For starters, I cursed and had a *very* negative attitude. I did not think good of anybody. I knew I had a problem. Scripture says, "But no man can tame the tongue. *It is* an unruly evil, full of deadly poison" (James 3:8). That scripture did not stop me from taking my potty mouth to the Lord, because I also knew Matthew 19:26 "But Jesus looked at *them* and said to them, 'With men this is impossible, but with God all things are possible.'"

Since the Spirit of God (the Holy Spirit who raised Jesus from the dead) lives in me, I decided to go to the Lord with my problem. I said, "Lord, I do not like the way I talk. I realize *I* cannot tame my tongue, so I give it to You to tame. Please teach me to speak only words that are life giving and glorifying, purge these curse words from me, in Jesus's name, amen."

My journey began with a simple testing. Each night, our girls would take a bath. I would say they were somewhere between three to four years old back then. While I sat on the couch, I would allow them to play in the tub together with their duckies, toys, colored soap paint, etc., because the couch had a clear shot to looking into the bathroom. The one rule I had was "If you want to splash each other, please shut the (clear) shower curtain so you don't get the floor wet."

For some reason, the "rule" kept getting forgotten. Anger would stir up in my veins and then the curse words would begin to spew out—"You s—— kids, what the h—— is the matter with you! Don't you listen? I said, Shut the freakin' curtain if you want to splash!"

With anger, I would be mumbling and grumbling as I would throw a towel on the floor to mop up the water. I was hot with anger. I knew this behavior in me was not godly, and I wanted help from the Holy Spirit. After each outburst, I would find myself going back into the bathroom, once I cool down, then repent to my girls and tell them, "Mom was wrong. That anger you just saw was not of God. I am sorry for getting so upset, please forgive me." My girls were looking at me with a deer in the headlight look, like I'm not sure as to what you are even saying. LOL.

Since I knew with God all things are possible, I made a pact with the Lord. "Lord, any time I am angry and getting ready to curse or speak anything that is not good, I am just going to speak in tongues. Holy Spirit, you need to get this anger out of me and tame my tongue, in Jesus's name, amen." Amen.

The first two weeks were the most intense. When the kids would test the principle by splashing, I would feel *great* anger rise up in me. I would look angry as could be and run into the bathroom, shut the shower curtain with great force, and I'd be yelling in tongues, then go to my bedroom and yell in tongues until peace came over me. For the first week, I was probably yelling in tongues for about one to two minutes at a time while crying, because I wanted this habit broken. I wanted the anger to no longer control me. After peace would come over me, I would go back into the bathroom, apologize to my kids once again, and explain to them not to splash when the curtain was open.

For weeks, this process went on, but the time of anger decreased from two minutes down to thirty seconds or so. One day, when the splashing happened again, the Lord said, "I want you to go in there [the bathroom] and laugh, just laugh."

I thought in my head: *Laugh? Are you kidding me? You want me to laugh at the water on the floor?*

Then the Lord said, "You are looking at this wrong. Laugh in the face of temptation. Now... go in there and laugh!" So with the fakest laugh ever, I went into the bathroom with a joker face smile and laughed and said, "I'm glad you are having fun, but let's just shut the curtain, okay?"

And with that, I shut the curtain and walked out. The girls were stunned. So the next stage was to laugh when it happened. I can tell you this, for starters, I had to force myself to smile and laugh, but as the weeks went on, it got easier and easier.

The whole process of that bathroom splashing experience took about three *solid* months of the Lord overhauling my soul man. Back then, I thought it was the cursing that was the root problem, but the real strong man in the situation was the spirit of anger. Anger was what made me react and swear. Once anger was dealt with, the cursing stopped. As I reflect on my life, that one incident was probably the most I gripped a hold of the Lord (like a Jacob's ladder) and was determined to be D-O-N-E with anger and cursing. I knew no man could tame a tongue, but the Holy Spirit can. I believe as I was praying in tongues, the Lord was ministering to me. The peace and loving kindness was so sweet as I would transition from anger to peace. The Holy Spirit is so gracious and merciful to help us in our weaknesses (Romans 8:26–27).

I was able to use that key principle of praying in tongues instead of swearing into other areas of my life while cooking in the kitchen. No longer would I get upset about dropping an onion on the floor by accident or spilling the milk, and other unimportant things. Anger just dissolved.

Will anger "try" to come back on me? It tries, but now, it is a familiar spirit. I can recognize its tactics and I shut it down, because I have been free from anger for so long, I never want to go back. If I forget to laugh, I go back to tongue talking. It is God talking to the situation/problem. I enjoy walking in peace, joy, and gladness now. I am free. So I encourage you, if you have an anger issue and it leads to cursing, ask the Holy Spirit to help you, hold onto Him, and pray in tongues. ☺

Scriptures referenced, New King James Version (NKJV)

Romans 8:26–27 Likewise the Spirit also helps in our weaknesses. For we do not know what we should pray for as we ought, but the Spirit Himself makes intercession for us with groanings which cannot be uttered. 27 Now He who searches the hearts knows what the mind of the Spirit *is,* because He makes intercession for the saints according to *the will of* God.

Being Translated and/or Visions

Many years ago, I was intrigued by Paul talking about someone being translated (moving through the atmosphere into another dimension) or whether it was a vision.

> ³And I know such a man—whether in the body or out of the body I do not know, God knows—⁴ how he was caught up into Paradise and heard inexpressible words, which it is not lawful for a man to utter. (2 Corinthians 12:3–4)

Another favorite of mine was Philip being translated in Acts 8:39–40

> ³⁹Now when they came up out of the water, the Spirit of the Lord caught Philip away, so that the eunuch saw him no more; and he went on his way rejoicing. ⁴⁰ But Philip was found at Azotus. And passing through, he preached in all the cities till he came to Caesarea.

I had said to the Lord, "I am open to be translated from one place to another and having cool visions." With that request, the Lord has granted me the opportunities. I will describe just a couple that are in correlation to praying in tongues. Some people may classify these as visions, so be it; whether it was a translating experience or just a vision, it is cool either way!

One day, I was exercising on my elliptical machine and I was praying in tongues and listening to music. As I began to pray, a strong Indian language came upon me. At first, the Indian language was funny to me, because it sounded like I was at an Indian Pow Wow. I busted out laughing. The Lord would gently say, "Come on... pray please." I would start again and bust out laughing again and again and again. My stomach was aching from the Indian chant song. I had tears of laughter rolling down my face, yet the Lord being ever so serious with me, "Come on, Tina, pray." After ten minutes of on/off prayer (because I found it so funny), I did get serious. I dove right into the prayer language, and I saw the Pow Wow. I could see the fire pit and people, and I just pressed in. The whole ordeal lasted about twenty minutes. I thought, *Wow, that was cool, I was translated!*

What was really cool is the next day, we were headed to the Upper Peninsula in Michigan to head to Wisconsin. We stopped at a hotel to rest for the night. When we pulled up to the hotel, there were two vehicles in the parking lot—ours and the desk clerk. As we are at the desk, I asked the clerk, "Can my grandparents and us have joining rooms, please?"

She responded, "Gee, I don't know. Let me check."

I said, "Are you kidding me? There are two vehicles in the parking lot—yours and ours. How can this be an issue?"

She responded, "We are booked tonight. There is an Indian Pow Wow going on down the street and all the Indians will be returning late tonight."

I let out a shout, "I was at the Pow Wow yesterday in the spirit!" I laughed to myself as others just looked at me strangely. I thought that was a cool experience.

I had another Indian Pow Wow experience at a ladies' retreat. During a time of praying in the spirit, three out of the eight of us were translated for a brief moment. That was *awesome*!

Another time of being translated happened during a time of intercessory prayer. In a gathering of a bunch of tongue-talking prayer warriors, we were praying in the spirit, and I was translated in the spirit or simply had a vision. I knew I was in the prayer room, but the room transformed into the pits of hell. I saw Satan at the center with a young teenage boy. In the spirit, I knew what to say, "RELEASE HIM! His grandmother is covered by the blood of Jesus. She is a praying woman and their line is saved for a thousand generations" (Deuteronomy 7:9). At that moment, the teenager was beside me. I turned to him and began to minister to him. He began to repent, and I lead him in a prayer of salvation. After that, I was back in the prayer room. I was so filled with joy and excitement; I sat down on the floor next to someone to tell them of the experience. Then, all of a sudden, I was being summoned to the court room of the Heavens. The prayer room disappeared again, and I was in a courtroom. I stood up and the boy was by my side. Satan was mad at me for demanding the boy from him and someone asked, "Who are you?"

I said with boldness, "I am a child of the Lord God Most High. This boy has a praying grandmother and their line is saved for a thousand generations." With that, a judge (I couldn't see the person; they were blurred) smacked down the gavel in our favor. "Case dismissed." Again, I was back in the prayer meeting. I was so excited. But wait there is more…

On the news the next day or so (no more the two days), there was a breaking news that a young teenage boy turned himself in. He was planning on doing a school shooting that week. I inquired of the

Lord about the situation because I was quickened in my spirit that was the boy in the vision. The school district was the same district my girlfriend's husband worked in. I just *love* how God looks out for *all* our loved ones and wants to expose and protect people and pull others away from the grips of Satan.

There are courtrooms in the heavens. This experience happened years ago and I was recently blessed by a man I saw on *It's Supernatural with Sid Roth*. The guest was named Robert Henderson; he has written a book on *Operating in the Courts of Heaven*. I listened to the CD version, and I was delighted to hear the confirmation of a similar experience.

When we pray in the spirit, please keep an open mind to be translated or enter into a vision. The Lord explained to me, "Forget your current surroundings and enter in." When He said "enter in," I knew what He meant. If you need to reach out and grab something in the spirit, do it in the natural. If you need to turn or walk to a different spot, do so. Forget about were your physical body may be and enter into the spiritual realm.

I realize this chapter may seem over the top for some, but for others, you *are* desiring to do the supernatural and help God out to redeem the times and pull people from the pits of hell. Jude 22–23 says,

> ²²And on some have compassion, making a distinction; ²³ but others save with fear, pulling them out of the fire, hating even the garment defiled by the flesh.

We need to partner with Jesus and be the voice piece to intercede for the saints. God has mysterious ways of getting the missions done while here on earth. As much as we need God, He needs us. We are to co-labor and partner with Him. God loves working with us and through us. It is a partnership, and when you see the answer to prayer, you rejoice together with Him and do a "High five! Great job! Mission complete. Let's go on the next adventure." God is not boring. There is plenty of work to get done. The prayers of the saints avails much (James 5:16). I truly believe that boy was spared through that time of intercession and what an honor it is to partner with God to save the boy and to protect my friend's husband and others. Amen and amen.

Scriptures referenced, New King James Version (NKJV)

Deuteronomy 7:9 Therefore know that the LORD your God, He *is* God, the faithful God who keeps covenant and mercy for a thousand generations with those who love Him and keep His commandments.

James 5:16 Confess *your* trespasses to one another, and pray for one another, that you may be healed. The effective, fervent prayer of a righteous man avails much.

Tongues in the Church

Up to now, I have been writing about the benefit package of speaking in tongues in your personal prayer life, also known as "praying in the Spirit." I like telling people about the personal prayer life benefits of tongues because the "tongues in the church" is such a touchy and misunderstood subject. There are two cooperate tongues that I will be addressing. The first is the tongues with interpretation for the purpose of prophecy. The second is a cooperate tongues for coming together in the unity of the Spirit for prayer or worship.

Let's look at 1 Corinthians 14:4–5

> [4]He who speaks in a tongue edifies himself, but he who prophesies edifies the church. [5] I wish you all spoke with tongues, but even more that you prophesied; for he who prophesies *is* greater than he who speaks with tongues, unless indeed he interprets, that the church may receive edification.

When you read this, please understand the setting Paul is writing to. He is writing to a "Church setting"—a group of people. The tongues mentioned here is different than the personal prayer life tongue. Yes, both are tongues, but this is a tongue prompted by the

Holy Spirit for the congregation, which will be interpreted, and not for an individual prayer life. In this group gathering, someone may speak loudly in tongues and someone else will interpret, "Thus saith the Lord..." The purpose of tongues and interpretation is to bring forth a prophecy. According to scripture, a prophecy should bring *edification, exhortation,* or *comfort* (1 Corinthians 14:3). Please look those words up in a dictionary to understand the full meaning of those words. I don't want to leave out a prophecy of warning like in the Old Testament.

You may ask, "How will you know the difference between the two tongues?" You just will. For example, when I was ready to deliver my daughter, I *just knew* and you will too. If the Holy Spirit ever prompts you to speak loudly in a church setting, most likely, it will be in a church that welcomes tongues and interpretation. God is a God of order and not disorder. If a church doesn't move in the gifts of the Spirit, it is unlikely you will ever be prompted there. The Holy Spirit knows if His presence is grieved by leadership or not.

When there is a multiple of people gathered together, there are a variety of needs, wants, and desires that need to get met. In 1 Corinthians 12:4–11,

> [4]There are diversities of gifts, but the same Spirit. [5]There are differences of ministries, but the same Lord. [6]And there are diversities of activities, but it is the same God who works all in all. [7]But the manifestation of the Spirit is given to each one for the profit *of all:* [8]for to one is given the word of wisdom through the Spirit, to another the word of knowledge through the same Spirit, [9]to another faith by the same Spirit, to another gifts of healings by the same Spirit, [10]to another the working of miracles, to another

prophecy, to another discerning of spirits, to another *different* kinds of tongues, to another the interpretation of tongues. [11] But one and the same Spirit works all these things, distributing to each one individually as He wills.

The Holy Spirit will move upon various people to manifest these gifts in the body of Christ to help profit all (vs. 7). One individual is not meant to help the whole masses. That is why the Holy Spirit will divide up the various gifts as needed. Please know, if you experienced the infilling of the Holy Spirit, you have the **whole** Holy Spirit not just a portion of the Spirit, therefore **all** the gifts mentioned above *can and will* flow through you *if* you so desire (Romans 8:11 and Psalm 37:4).

God wants His children healed, made well, and prospering. When there are a bunch of true believers gathered together, the gifts flow as the Holy Spirit wills. Since one may speak in tongues and another interpret, and another have a word of wisdom, etc., it is about "working together." God *loves* it when we each do a part to help the whole. He is like a great coach or a director of a play. He wants everyone to partake, so no one feels left out. He is proud of all His children and wants them to shine. For instance, my daughter was in a play at school and she had a small part in the performance, but it was necessary and sufficient. It wasn't the leading role, but it was needed to make the play a success, just like all the people behind the scenes doing the props, lighting, sound, etc. God wants **everyone** to have a part in our gatherings, because it can flow so beautifully.

I want to make this clear by repeating myself once again: if you work in a gift, let's say healing, that is not the only gift that you have in you. You have the Holy Spirit. You have the whole Holy Spirit in you, not just a piece of the Holy Spirit. Therefore, *ALL* the gifts are available—KNOW that truth! Don't limit God by your belief system. Allow Him to work *ALL* of the gifts of the Holy Spirit in and through you to the people. Myself and others flow in all the gifts. It is obtainable, because you have the whole Holy Spirit. ☺

One of the most common misconceptions about tongues is that "tongues only happen as the Spirit wills." That is correct *in the church setting*. Tongues in general is for *every believer*. You can look at the book of Acts. I love the scripture from Mark 16:15–18 when Jesus is speaking and tells his disciples (if you have a Catholic Bible, it may be omitted):

> [15]And He said to them, "Go into all the world and preach the gospel to every creature.[16] He who believes and is baptized will be saved; but he who does not believe will be condemned.[17] **And these signs will follow those who believe**: In My name they will cast out demons; **they will speak with new tongues**;[18] they will take up serpents; and if they drink anything deadly, it will by no means hurt them; they will lay hands on the sick, and they will recover."

Isn't that wonderful! Every believer should have the signs of tongues manifested in their life! ☺ Tongues is multifaceted, and until you start working in it, you will not get the total revelation. It is like a person who gives birth to a child; you quickly learn that parenting out of book and parenting in reality are much different. You gain experiential knowledge and you gain an unshakable understanding of parenting; the same is true with tongues as you partake in it.

In conclusion to tongues in the church setting, do not speak in tongues loudly *on your own* in hopes of interpretation that it is going to benefit the church. You have to be prompted by the Holy Spirit to *know* He has a word for the church. Trust me, you will "know" if He is wanting you to speak loudly for everyone to hear. One side note here: please make sure you know the portal call of the church guidelines about whether or not tongues and interpretation is allowed or not. If the pastor/priest/minister does not want tongues and interpretation to be done aloud, PLEASE respect their guidelines. Again, God is a God of order. Submit to the governing authorities. If you feel you have a Word, see if you can talk to leadership on the side to get permission. Be orderly and respectful of the church policies.

When I first started speaking in tongues, I really wanted the church I attended to receive these great gifts, but leadership did not believe in them. I went through a period of rebellion till the Lord calmed me down to explain to me, "a sower sows the seed." I was there to help bring revelation to the leadership (politely), if they didn't want to accept it, that was not my fault. I was just the messenger of the good news. There are other incidents where I spoke to leadership, and they did believe in tongues and interpretation, but they just didn't want the manifestation at their building. You have to respect leadership's decision. You don't have to like the decision, but let the Holy Spirit teach them the beauty of it—pray diligently for leadership. If a non-tongue talking church wants no part in it, ask the Lord if you can go elsewhere. (Please make sure you read the chapter on "God wants a pizza.")

I pray as you read through 1 Corinthians 12–14 and other scriptures, you will allow the Holy Spirit to teach you the difference between corporate tongues and personal prayer life. In the next couple chapters, I will discuss cooperate prayer, singing in the Spirit, and the unity of Spirit.

Scriptures referenced, New King James Version (NKJV)

Psalm 37:4 Delight yourself also in the LORD, And He shall give you the desires of your heart.

Romans 8:11 But if the Spirit of Him who raised Jesus from the dead dwells in you, He who raised Christ from the dead will also give life to your mortal bodies through His Spirit who dwells in you.

1 Corinthians 14:3 But he who prophesies speaks edification and exhortation and comfort to men.

Corporate Prayer

I had the privilege of being mentored in a spirit-filled environment of awesome prayer warriors shortly after I got baptized in the Holy Spirit (speaking in tongues). As we gathered together for Bible study/prayer meeting, we would be praying in tongues at a low rumble. Since this group of prayer warriors were of "like precious faith" (Philippians 2:2) and "in the unity of the Spirit," we did not think it odd to all pray out the mysterious amongst each other (1 Corinthians 14:2). As the low rumble of tongues was sounding, someone else would be praying in our native tongue, English, and occasionally we would chime in and say "amen" or add to the prayer as needed. The Bible says, when two or more come together in agreement it is done (Matthew 18:18–20). There was order in the prayer meeting and it flowed so smoothly. Even today, in some select prayer meetings, we operate in this type of harmony and unity.

As we pray, I can sense interpretation of tongues going on. We all have the ability to interpret our tongues or others; it's just a matter of asking the Lord to open that gift. According to 1 Corinthians 14:13, "Therefore let him who speaks in a tongue pray that he may interpret." I want to point this out that "pray that he may interpret." If someone is praying in tongues, you also have the ability to interpret; otherwise, Paul would not be encouraging people to "pray that he may interpret." In some church settings, there is a mind-set that a person can only operate in one gift. That is a false teaching. We are to operate in *all* the gifts of the Holy Spirit, because we have the fullness **of** the Holy Spirit. You did not receive just a small portion. You received everything. Christ is also in you and He operated in various gifts all the time.

There is one more beautiful form of praying together in tongues that is rare and very unique. It is praying in one accord, which I will discuss in the chapter "One Accord, Unity of the Spirit."

I have been in (tongue talking) prayer meetings where it is just pure chaos. A few people are yelling in tongues, others are praying softly, another is singing in the Spirit, and another one or two may be yelling out prayers in the native tongue (English). Ugh! I always felt sorry for newbies coming to this prayer meeting. It was more like a shouting match. Who can shout the loudest to be heard for someone to agree and say "Amen." One thing I know is God is not deaf, nor are the angels. I understand there is a warring in the Spirit (a warlike tongue on occasion), but it is different than a prideful tongue that just wants to be heard. Even though those types of meetings are like a loud gong, I do believe there is something of good going on, because they are all speaking the language of God and the angels. Therefore, angels are being dispatched to do something, but honestly, I do not sense harmony or unity in those type of meetings.

I personally prefer the more harmonious tongue-talking prayer meetings where the tongues is at a low rumble and we are listening to one another and agreeing as someone speaks in English as well. Many times during a smooth flowing prayer meeting, we end up singing in the unity of the Spirit.

Scriptures referenced, New King James Version (NKJV)

Matthew 18:18–20 [18]"Assuredly, I say to you, whatever you bind on earth will be bound in heaven, and whatever you loose on earth will be loosed in heaven.[19] "Again I say to you that if two of you agree on earth concerning anything that they ask, it will be done for them by My Father in heaven.[20] For where two or three are gathered together in My name, I am there in the midst of them."

1 Corinthians 14:2 For he who speaks in a tongue does not speak to men but to God, for no one understands *him;* however, in the spirit he speaks mysteries.

Philippians 2:2 (Amplified) Fill up *and* complete my joy by living in harmony *and* being of the same mind *and* one in purpose, having the same love, being in full accord and of one harmonious mind *and* intention.

Singing in the Spirit

In a harmonious prayer meeting or worship service, most likely, the believers will end up singing in the Spirit. Singing corporately in the Spirit can be done whenever/wherever there are believers of like precious faith. John 4:23–24:

> 23But the hour is coming, and now is, when the true worshipers will worship the Father in spirit and truth; for the Father is seeking such to worship Him. 24God *is* Spirit, and those who worship Him must worship in spirit and truth.

The Lord is looking for His children to worship Him in spirit and truth. During a spirit-filled worship, there is a harmonizing in tongues. It is like we are each a separate instrument in a symphony and yet we blend so beautifully together. It is a song from the heart (Colossians 3:16 and Ephesians 5:19). There have been times a trumpet blast will sound from my belly and through my vocal cords that will sound just like a shofar blowing. It is awesome! Each one of us carry a sound, a frequency. Each frequency changes the course of matter/structure.

I encourage you to let loose when you are in a charismatic environment so you can experience God. (I worship in tongues even throughout the day when I'm driving, taking a shower, cleaning house, etc.) I do enjoy group gatherings of worship in the spirit the most. I feel like we are a big family singing to Abba Father and He is so delighted with all of us working together to praise Him with a new song. He *wants* us to sing to Him a new song (Psalm 149:1 and many other scriptures). ☺

On occasion, you will sense the Lord singing a song to you through your voice. This is a song from the Lord like in Zephaniah 3:17, where He will rejoice over us with singing; it's a song not from human writings—not a man-made song. Songs from the Lord can really minister *love* to you, like you've never known before.

I had just briefly mentioned above about frequencies and our voice being a sound. I love the studies done by Dr. Masaru Emoto and Caroline Leaf and others. They show the importance of words (vibrations). Vibrations can change a matter/substance. I recommend you check into these other resources to get it settled in your spirit how important each word we speak is life changing. The scriptures say, "Death and life *are* in the power of the tongue, and those who love it will eat its fruit" (Psalm 18:21). Your words are like a ready writer (Psalm 45:1). You will speak forth your destiny. That is why Jesus continually said, "ask", "speak," or "say" to your circumstances (Mark 11:22–24). There is an action (words) that *must* be spoken out of our mouths in order to bring it into existence. We are made in the image of God, therefore we do likewise. God spoke the universe into existence. We are His children, we do likewise and *speak.* Our tongue may be a small member of our body, but it is very strong, and it will guide us into a life of abundance or lack, just as scripture says in James 3:3–5

> ³ Indeed, we put bits in horses' mouths that they may obey us, and we turn their whole body. ⁴ Look also at ships: although they are so

large and are driven by fierce winds, they are turned by a very small rudder wherever the pilot desires. 5 Even so the tongue is a little member and boasts great things. See how great a forest a little fire kindles!

The tongue is such a small member of the body, but it is the life-giving substance that either tares down or builds up. As we join together in cooperate gatherings, let's learn to harmonize, listen, speak, and sing.

Scriptures referenced, New King James Version (NKJV)

Zephaniah 3:17 "The LORD your God in your midst,
The Mighty One, will save;
He will rejoice over you with gladness,
He will quiet *you* with His love,
He will rejoice over you with singing."

Psalm 45:1 My heart is overflowing with a good theme;
I recite my composition concerning the King;
My tongue *is* the pen of a ready writer.

Psalm 149:1 Praise the LORD! Sing to the LORD a new song,
And His praise in the assembly of saints.

Mark 11:22–24 22 So Jesus answered and said to them, "Have faith in God.23 For assuredly, I say to you, whoever says to this mountain, 'Be removed and be cast into the sea,' and does not doubt in his heart, but believes that those things he says will be done, he will have whatever he says.24 Therefore I say to you, whatever things you ask when you pray, believe that you receive *them,* and you will have *them.*

Colossians 3:16 Let the word of Christ dwell in you richly in all wisdom, teaching and admonishing one another in psalms and hymns and spiritual songs, singing with grace in your hearts to the Lord.

Ephesians 5:19 Speaking to one another in psalms and hymns and spiritual songs, singing and making melody in your heart to the Lord.

Unity in the Spirit, One Accord

My first experience with one accord happened when I gathered together with another sister in Christ. We were planning a twenty-four-hour tongue talking day. Our plan was to eat only fruits and veggies and pray in tongues for most of the time. We were doing great! What was so cool is we experienced a "unity in the spirit." As we prayed in tongues, we began speaking the same thing at the same time! We could discern certain languages like French, Asian, and lots of Indian languages. As we pressed on, it was like we were traveling around the world with different languages. When we would linger in a language that was when the one accord would happen. Here is one definition of the word *accord*[1]: to make, agree or harmonize; reconcile; mutual agreement; harmony.

As we spoke in tongues, neither one of us knew the next word, but the Holy Spirit did, because He is *in* both of us. I think of the harmonizing as the Lord's voice being *magnified*. Magnify the Lord with me and exalt His name forever (Psalm 34:3). We were defi-

---

[1]   Neufeldt, Victoria and Guralnik, David B., *Webster's New World Dictionary*, Third College Edition of American English, Simon & Schuster Inc. 1988.

nitely magnifying the Lord together, because it is His Holy Spirit (His Language) being spoken in and through us. As God said, "Light be," light was (Genesis 1:3). Therefore when we speak in tongues, it is Him (God) speaking through us as we yield to the Holy Spirit. Another point to make is when Matthew 18:19–20 when Jesus is speaking:

> [19]Again I say to you that if <u>two</u> of you <u>agree</u> on earth concerning anything that they ask, <u>it will be done</u> for them by My Father in heaven. [20]For where two or three are gathered together in My name, I am there in the midst of them.

I love that scripture! When we come into one accord, we can break some spiritual Jericho walls down with a sound of unity (Joshua 6).

There are problems that sometimes arise in larger groups, though. There must be a complete surrender, a submitting, one to another in order for it to be successful. I have found in larger groups, pride and haughtiness to be a stopping factor for one accord. I cannot describe the experience any other way then "you must submit one to another." I have heard one person say, "Oh, not THAT language again, I don't want to pray in *that* language." That grieved me when they refused to pray out that particular language. They would grieve the Holy Spirit (Ephesians 4:30). The tongue may be an odd language to us, but apparently, it is a language in God's realm or in the nations.

If you don't come into *one accord*, you can definitely tap into the same languages through submission. Just listen to the dominate language being spoken in tongues and join in. If you have a few people, you will sense the Holy Spirit move from one person to the next, in no particular order. I like to think of this like white water rafting (even though I've never been, except in my mind)... the Holy

Spirit will just flow like a river and we are in the boat. As you listen, just tap into a language together and hopefully everyone else will join in. Sometimes the language is soft and gently like a smooth stream, then other times it is harsh and warring like rough waters and like a fight. Pray it through until there is *peace*. After one tongue gets *peace*, listen, as everyone is in a low rumble of tongues and wait for the next dominate tongue to arise, then jump into the next river. The unity consists of flowing, listening, and submitting.

I inquired of this unity of the spirit and one accord with the Lord one day. I asked, "Lord, what is this all about?" There were three points: (1) His voice is magnified (Psalm 34:3); (2) like the walls of Jericho coming down, when they all came in one accord and the walls fell; (3) it is the word *fabricate*. I put the brakes on right there. Fabricate? What does that mean? Is that something negative like a lie? The Lord laughed and said, "Look it up."

So I was led back to the dictionary. (When you walk with the Lord, you have three main books: the Bible, a concordance, and a good dictionary.) According to the *Webster's New World Dictionary*, the first definition is the one He wanted me to focus in on:

Fabricate[2]: 1. to make, build, construct, etc. esp. by assembling parts; manufacture.

He had me mediate on "to make, build, construct, manufacture." As we come together in the one accord, God is in the midst and it is *done*. God knows what to do and how to manufacture the creative miracles. He just needs our voice to "Get R Done."

I said, "Lord, I haven't heard anyone teach on these truths." He said, "These are the new wine skins." The old traditional people will not accept these truths.

---

[2]   Neufeldt, Victoria and Guralnik, David B., *Webster's New World Dictionary*, Third College Edition of American English, Simon & Schuster Inc. 1988.

And no one puts new wine into old wineskins; or else the new wine bursts the wineskins, the wine is spilled, and the wineskins are ruined. But new wine must be put into new wineskins. (Mark 2:22)

I said, "Okay, Lord. For those who are willing, we will pray in one accord and magnify your name." Shortly after the unveiling of this type of prayer, the Lord lead me to an awesome teaching by a wonderful prayer warrior, and she, too, taught on one accord. I thank God for confirmations.

Scriptures referenced, New King James Version (NKJV)

Genesis 1:3 Then God said, "Let there be light"; and there was light.

Psalm 34:3 Oh, magnify the Lord with me, And let us exalt His name together.

Ephesians 4:30 And do not grieve the Holy Spirit of God, by whom you were sealed for the day of redemption.

How Do You Receive?

Before receiving the Holy Spirit, there needs to be an acceptance of making Jesus your Lord and Savior (Romans 10:9). Then there is the receiving of the Holy Spirit (John 7:38–39). I love what Paul says in Acts 19:1–6 (New Living Translation):

> While Apollos was in Corinth, Paul traveled through the interior regions until he reached Ephesus, on the coast, where he found several believers. ² "Did you receive the Holy Spirit when you believed?" he asked them.
>
> "No," they replied, "we haven't even heard that there is a Holy Spirit."
>
> ³ "Then what baptism did you experience?" he asked.
>
> And they replied, "The baptism of John."
>
> ⁴ Paul said, "John's baptism called for repentance from sin. But John himself told the people to

believe in the one who would come later, meaning Jesus."

[5] As soon as they heard this, they were baptized
in the name of the Lord Jesus. [6] Then when Paul
laid his hands on them, the Holy Spirit came
on them, and they spoke in other tongues and
prophesied.

I want you to see there are two separate transactions here: (1) to
receive Jesus as Lord, and (2) to receive the Holy Spirit.

When we look at Jesus, Jesus commanded the disciples in Acts
1:4, "And being assembled together with *them,* He **commanded**
them not to depart from Jerusalem, but to **wait** for the Promise of
the Father..." This was no small request; it was a command. When
you read the book of Acts chapter 2, you will see that 120 people
came together and waited for the Holy Spirit to come. Praise be to
God, He did. The good news for us is, we don't have to wait for the
Holy Spirit to come. He's here now. We just need to receive Him by
faith. Ask and you shall receive (John 16:24).

Jesus continues on and said in Acts 1:8, "But you shall receive
power when the Holy Spirit has come **upon** you; and you shall be
witnesses to Me in Jerusalem, and in all Judea and Samaria, and to
the end of the earth."

Let's first focus in on that word *power.* In Greek, that word
for *power* is the Greek word *dunamis.*[3] *Dunamis* (1411) is a miracu-
lous power: ability, abundance, meaning mighty worker of miracle.
Dunamis is the root word of our English word *dynamite.* When we
receive the Holy Spirit, we receive dynamite to blow Satan and his

---

[3]   Strong, James, *Strong's Comprehensive Concordance of the Bible with
       Hebrew Chaldee and Greek Dictionaries,* World Bible Publishers, Inc.,
       ISBN 0-529-06334-3.

tactics up. Satan wants to steal, kill, and destroy us, but Jesus came to give us life and life more abundantly (John 10:10). Thank you, Jesus! Now, let's look at the word *upon*.

Upon is two words, "up" and "on." The Holy Spirit will come UP out of your belly, where He resides, and up through your vocal cords (tongues), out into the atmosphere and you will hear it. The words will go back ON you and into your ear gates and circle back through your body. UP and ON you, **upon** you. Isn't that glorious?! I love that.

To receive the infilling of the Holy Spirit (tongues), make sure the person has received Jesus as their Lord and Savior. Then do a prayer to receive the Holy Spirit. I usually start with a prayer like, "Lord, we bind all principalities of darkness right now. We loosen you, Lord, to have liberty here. Lord, fill (person's name) with your Holy Spirit. (Person's name), receive ye now the Holy Spirit." I lightly blow on them like Jesus did (John 20:22). Then I have them recite a prayer, "Lord, I receive Jesus as my Lord and Savior, fill me now with your Holy Spirit, so I may speak in tongues, amen." I then wait for them to speak in tongues, as I softly pray in the Spirit.

About 40 percent of the people I pray with will begin to start speaking right away. Then there are others, the 60 percent, that are very mind conscious and are being exposed to tongues for the first time, and they don't know how to connect to the Well within. If no spiritual language begins to bubble up after a while, I offer to them to "Just pick something. Pick a dadadadada, or a mamamamama, or tatatatatata or any syllable and start to repeat it. Not from your mind, but from your spirit."

They are not to talk their native tongue, because they will *think* about what they are saying. Some will try to repeat, "Jesus, Jesus, Jesus." I stop them. The Holy Spirit's language is different and the native tongue is going to stop the flow from happening. God's ways are higher. We are obtaining God's language, heaven's language, so we need to be submissive to learn His language. There needs to be an initiation (activation) on the believer's part to allow the Holy Spirit to manifest. They cannot remain silent. As they work in the dada-dada (or whatever they choose), I spiritually discern if there are any hangups. Do they feel unworthy? If so, I stop the process and explain to them just how *worth it* they are. Jesus died for them. I usually give it a minute. Then I may say, "Drop it down from your mind to your spirit" or "Lord, we loosen the tongue, in Jesus's name, amen." Each and every person is different.

When I am praying with someone, it helps that they speak loud enough for me to hear them. Again, they cannot be silent. They must speak. I have found that if they speak at the normal tone level while receiving, the process is fairly quick. It has to do with them "hearing." If they are very soft, it takes forever or it just won't happen. Normal tone volume is good. No need to scream or get too loud. As they work with the syllables of choice, I can hear other syllables start to gather and I encourage them, "There it is… keep it going… Yes, Lord, more, more, amen."

Once they get the full manifestation of tongues (more than the dadadada, mamama, but a full language going), they *may* breakdown, shake, cry, shout, yell, and holler with glee but no need to shout when activating. Afterward, bring it on, let the party begin! Rejoice! Be glad! ☺

Many people think, "Oh, I spoke in tongues once a long time ago, I'm good." That is a misconception. A long time ago was just that, a long time ago; you need to be renewing your mind daily in tongues. Remember, when you speak in tongues, you are speaking the oracles of God and angels. God's word will not return void; it *will* accomplish where it is sent (Isaiah 55:11). You are also speaking "mysteries" (1 Corinthians 14:2). The Lord gave me this vision of angels standing at attention, waiting for someone to speak their language so they can go to work for the day to make our way straight. As we speak in tongues (their language), the angels dispatch. Remember the Holy Spirit speaks only what the Father says in John 16:13,

> However, when He, the Spirit of truth, has come, He will guide you into all truth; for He will not speak on His own *authority,* but whatever He hears He will speak; and He will tell you things to come.

So the Holy Spirit is speaking what He hears the Father speak. It is pure; it is untainted. It will not return void. That is so powerful. I love releasing the oracles of God into the atmosphere. As you work in tongues, sometimes you will know what you are praying about. You may hear a certain name or city come up as you pray, just be encouraged that those words going forth are availing much.

There is a religious idea out there at is a pure cop out of why certain people have not partaken in the gift of tongues. The cop out goes like this: "Well, when it is time for me, then the Lord will just make it happen. I'm not going to force the issue." First of all, scripture says in John 16:24, "Until now you have asked nothing in My name. Ask, and you will receive, that your joy may be full". You must "ask" and you will "receive." There is an initiation process in order to make it happen. God is all about manifesting His presence in people's lives. He hungers and desires to be one with us, but we need to come to Him first (John 14:20–21).

Be encouraged today. Pray and sing in tongues. Be sure to stir up the gift while getting ready in the morning, driving your vehicle, cleaning house or whenever you can. Also, tell others about this glorious gift. Encourage people that Holy Spirit and tongues will help them. I like to give them this statement for mediation, "If you go to France, it is helpful to speak French. If you go to Spain, it's helpful to speak Spanish. If you want to tap into the heavenlies, it's helpful to speak God's language, tongues. Yes, you can get along in life without it, but how much better you can have life if you know the language."

As you tell others and work in this gift, together, we will "take this land back for our Lord Jesus Christ" (this was a saying the Lord has me continuously decree for years now).

Scriptures referenced, New King James Version (NKJV)

Isaiah 55:11 So shall My word be that goes forth from My mouth;
It shall not return to Me void,
But it shall accomplish what I please,
And it shall prosper *in the thing* for which I sent it.

John 7:38–39 [38] He who believes in Me, as the Scripture has said, out of his heart will flow rivers of living water."[39] But this He spoke concerning the Spirit, whom those believing in Him would receive; for the Holy Spirit was not yet *given,* because Jesus was not yet glorified.

John 10:10 The thief does not come except to steal, and to kill, and to destroy. I have come that they may have life, and that they may have *it* more abundantly.

John 14:20–21 [20]At that day you will know that I *am* in My Father, and you in Me, and I in you.[21] He who has My commandments and keeps them, it is he who loves Me. And he who loves Me will be loved by My Father, and I will love him and manifest Myself to him."

John 16:24 Until now you have asked nothing in My name. Ask, and you will receive, that your joy may be full.

John 20:22 And when He had said this, He breathed on *them,* and said to them, "Receive the Holy Spirit."

1 Corinthians 14:2 For he who speaks in a tongue does not speak to men but to God, for no one understands *him;* however, in the spirit he speaks mysteries.

Romans 10:9 That if you confess with your mouth the Lord Jesus and believe in your heart that God has raised Him from the dead, you will be saved.

God Wants a Pizza

Interesting title isn't it? "God wants a pizza." It came as a shocker to me too when the Lord said that to me. This chapter is not about a mystery of tongues, but it holds a very important truth you need to keep in mind, as you may work in tongues and others do not.

One day, I was bashing the Catholics. I was a former Catholic, and I felt I didn't learn about the Lord, Bible studies, Jesus, and the Holy Spirit like I thought I should have. I was complaining to God, "Rituals! Rituals! That's all I learned from them…" From there, I bashed a different church, because they didn't believe in speaking in tongues. My list of negativity about one church then another was starting to roll, when the Lord interpreted my bashing party.

The Lord asked, "Do you know what I want?"

I said, "No. What?"

He said, "I want a pizza with everything on it."

As I shook my head in disbelief, I responded, "Excuse me? I'm bashing the churches and you want a pizza?"

The Lord's response, "Yes, a pizza. The bread is the foundation, My Word, the very substance everything is going to lay upon. The sauce is the Blood of my Son that covers My Word. The cheese, that is the Holy Spirit that binds everything together, again, covering My Word and the Blood of Jesus. Do you know what I want on my pizza?"

After a response like that, I was blown away and just shook my head "no."

"I want everything on my pizza. Mushrooms, pepperonis, green peppers, anchovies—everything! Because each topping represents a church—Methodist, Pentecostal, Lutheran, Catholic, etc. And I want my pizza loaded, so no matter where I cut that slice (triangular)—Father, Son, Holy Spirit—and bite into it, all the flavors are working together. It is a sweet savor to my mouth." He went on to explain, "You all know in part. This church over here… they are feeding the people of Flint. Yah, they don't raise their hands during worship, but I am well pleased. This church over there… yah, they don't believe in tongues, but they are clothing the people of Flint. These Catholics… they are trying to please me by the recitals because they are shadowing the Jewish customs (baby dedications = baby baptism, bar mitzvah = confirmations, priests, etc.). Their heart is to please me and it does. When the body of Christ works together, it pleases me."

I was floored. From that day forward, I am determined to love the people in the church and encourage them to keep on keeping on. Yes, there is a desire for the churches to come into a unity of the faith and there is a time coming when the Holy Spirit will be received in *all* the churches (the former and latter rains), but until then, "Love each other as I love you" (John 13:34–35).

Give God a pizza. Work together in the body of Christ. ☺

Scriptures referenced, New King James Version (NKJV)

John 13:34–35 [34] "A new commandment I give to you, that you love one another; as I have loved you, that you also love one another. [35] By this all will know that you are My disciples, if you have love for one another."

About the Author

Tina Jackson is dedicated to informing people of the love of God. She is the editor, producer, and host of *U Beautiful Creation*, a Christian-based talk show located in Michigan and available to view on YouTube. Tina desires to see the Body of Christ come together in one accord and understand the mysteries of God's ways.

CPSIA information can be obtained
at www.ICGtesting.com
Printed in the USA
FFOW03n1455170617
36712FF